UNDERSTANDING
Your 4 year old

UNDERSTANDING
Your 4 year old

Lisa Miller

of the

TAVISTOCK CLINIC

Series Editor: Elsie Osborne

ROSENDALE PRESS

Copyright © 1992 The Tavistock Clinic

First published in Great Britain in 1992 by
Rosendale Press Ltd
Premier House, 10 Greycoat Place
London SW1P 1SB
Reprinted 1993, 1994, 1997

Design by Pep Reiff
Production Edward Allhusen
Typesetting Ace Filmsetting Ltd
Printed in Great Britain by The Cromwell Press
Broughton Gifford, Wiltshire

British Library Cataloguing in Publication Data
A catalogue record for this book is available from
The British Library

ISBN 1 872803 25 3

The Tavistock Clinic, London, was founded in 1920, in order to meet the needs of people whose lives had been disrupted by the First World War. Today, it is still committed to understanding people's needs though, of course, times and people have changed. Now, as well as working with adults and adolescents, the Tavistock Clinic has a large department for children and families. This offers help to parents who are finding the challenging task of bringing up their children daunting and has, therefore, a wide experience of children of all ages. It is firmly committed to early intervention in the inevitable problems that arise as children grow up, and to the view that if difficulties are caught early enough, parents are the best people to help their children with them.

Professional Staff of the Clinic were, therefore, pleased to be able to contribute to this series of books to describe the ordinary development of children, to help in spotting the growing pains and to provide ways that parents might think about their children's growth.

THE AUTHOR

Lisa Miller worked as a teacher after leaving university at Oxford. She trained as a child psycho-therapist at the Tavistock Clinic, London, where she now works in the Department of Children and Families. Her time is divided between clinical work and teaching; and she is responsible for the Under-Fives Counselling Service which offers up to five interviews for any parent or parent-to-be concerned about a baby or small child.

Her publications include editorship (with Margaret Rustin, Michael Rustin and Judy Shuttleworth) of "Closely observed infants": an account of the method of infant observation pioneered at the Tavistock.

Lisa Miller is married with four children.

CONTENTS

INTRODUCTION

Many people, looking back, find that their conscious memories begin in a continuous way from some time between their fourth and fifth birthdays. We can recall isolated incidents or feelings from before this age; but it is from about this year onwards that most of us could start to write some kind of autobiography. We could combine what we have been told by others with what we remember ourselves to form a more or less continuous narrative of our lives. Perhaps this implies that around this age we develop a feeling of being ourselves; and this certainly corresponds with the way in which children at this age are consolidating their elementary feelings of being separate people from their parents. An old lady, looking back, said that she felt she had not changed essentially from the time when she as a four-year-old was taken to have her photograph taken for her father who was fighting in the war. She could recall in detail having discovered that there are two sorts of smiles, one that you just do, and one that you put on deliberately. She rather suspected her "deliberate" smile, and was surprised when the grown-ups were more than satisfied by it for photographic purposes.

We can see here a small girl who was most observant of herself and the people around her, who thought for herself and who kept things to herself, and who was storing things away to last for eighty years. We do not know now what the meaning of the event was which caused it to be so well-remembered; however, we know that this small girl's mother took her to be photographed for her father. Here we have a hint of what is of prime importance to all four-year-olds: the relationship they have with the principal adults in their lives, and in particular with their fathers and mothers. A small baby relates to one person at a time, but at the time of weaning the notion of a third person comes into mind. The baby gets a feeling that his mother (or his principal care-giver) is no longer putting him absolutely first in her mind. Rivals jostle for place. Could it be that mummy has a connection with somebody else? Could daddy be a candidate?

By the time that the girl or boy reaches four years old, this question has been mulled over, answered, and re-answered for a long time. The four year old is deeply interested in relationships – in relationships between children and parents, between child and father or child and mother, between any two adults, between father and mother. The four-year-old is thinking these things out in a way which, as we shall see, underlies a good many of the typical reactions and preoccupations of his or her age. No matter how important relationships with siblings or friends may be (and of course they can be very important) a four-year-old is still in a primary fashion concerned first with the adults in his life, and second with the children.

CHAPTER ONE

THE DEVELOPMENT OF RELATIONSHIPS

Mothers and fathers

The four-year-old is continuing to work away at fundamental questions connected with how he or she sees his or her mother and father and the relationship between them. Even when there is only one parent actually in the home, the fact remains that you need two people to make a child, and that child (as I shall discuss later) will use all the ingenuity and information at his or her disposal to think about mothers if he or she is being brought up by father or about fathers if it is his mother he or she lives with and knows better.

Investigating this simple fact – that every child must somewhere have two parents – is so important that it seems to underlie many other complex and far-reaching ideas which a child is developing about how things connect up with each other to allow something new to form. It's happening all over the place. You see something on the television, it connects up with your mind, and a question or an idea is formed. You put a small plant in the garden and it connects up with the soil and a big bushy one grows. If you are four you get together with a friend and have an idea about what to play. If you're playing by yourself you join up with your Lego or bricks or cars and make something of it. Our capacity to think is inseparable from our capacity to make connections.

So here we have four-year-olds preoccupied (sometimes consciously, sometimes at the remoter levels of their minds) with connections. They will have mixed feelings about it. For the whole notion of a connection and a new idea is a powerful one, just as is the notion that mummy and daddy can get together as a couple and do things which the four-year-old cannot be part of. Sometimes the idea of mummy and daddy together gives the child a nice feeling of happiness and harmony. Sometimes the child feels left out, cross, and either jealous or envious. Allowing the parents to be together without upsetting or disturbing them makes some demands on the generosity and resources of a small child. But it is important that it should happen – that the child should be able to leave his or her parents to get on with things together, without the feeling it is unbearable if he or she isn't there too.

Caroline was a forceful little girl, passionately attached to both her parents. She went out for the afternoon with her grandmother and when she came back she went into the sitting room. Her father and mother didn't hear them arrive through the garden door, and were still sitting close together on the sofa by a low table when she rushed in. They were the picture of intimacy; they had been looking through catalogues and paint-samples and with a great deal of agreement planning house decorations. They looked up and smiled. But for some reason to do with what was happening in her own mind, Caroline didn't respond with pleasure. She hovered as if she didn't know which one to hug. She moved over to the table and began to ask, "What's that?" in a suspicious way about the catalogue pictures. Her parents began to explain about new shelves and cupboards: Caroline kicked the table and said she didn't want any. She started to mess about with the bits of paper in an irritating way. Her parents' efforts to interest her soon got lost as they told her to leave things alone. She went on whining, "What's that? I don't like it – don't want it . . ." until her mother got cross and said, "Well, Caroline, I like it, *we* like it, we think it's very nice, now come on and have tea." She took Caroline's hand rather brusquely; Caroline burst into tears, started saying "No, no," and quite a tantrum ensued. What had gone wrong?

It seems as though a thought had struck Caroline when she came back to see her parents together, a thought which might be something like, "What have they been doing without *me*?" Also, the warmth of the connection between them reminded her of how warmly she felt about each one of them. Did she want to hug Mummy, and push Daddy away? or did she want to claim Daddy and exclude Mummy? If she were to greet them both together, that would involve acknowledging that they formed a sort of unit, a combination called a couple. No matter how much that couple loved her – and indeed, they had been spending some of their time thinking about her and planning nice things for her as well as for themselves – Caroline still felt acutely that they were grown up, different from herself and capable of doing things which she couldn't do. She had realised that while she was out with Granny, her parents had gone on existing. They had been living their lives in her absence. She could not control them and neither could she always know what they did.

This was one side of Caroline's reaction. Another side was shown a few weeks later. For the first time, her parents were spending a night away from home without her, and she was to go to Granny's. On this occasion Caroline felt predominantly pleased and excited, confident that Granny and Grandpa could look after her nicely, feeling big and independent. As her parents were saying goodbye from their car, Caroline called out, "Goodbye! Have lots of lovely luxury!" Everybody laughed, her mother jumped out and kissed her and said, "Thank you, darling", her grandparents murmured about how clever she was and where did she get such words, and the farewells took place in a most cheerful spirit.

We can see that Caroline is still a very dominant little personality and throws her own contribution into the scene in a marked fashion. Maybe in her imagination her parents were off on a fairytale expedition, and maybe also in her imagination she was off on it too. But in another way she was content to stay behind and to relish what was there for her. And she made a point of uttering good wishes, hoping that her parents would have a lovely time, using this grown-up word "luxury" which was her attempt to conceptualise something extra-special and a bit outside her own experience.

Caroline does not want to spoil her parents' pleasure. That is to say, since spoiling is the trademark of envy, she is trying not to be envious. Of course, I do not mean that she is thinking it out consciously. It is sometimes hard to imagine how much of our thinking is done deep down in our minds at a level of which we simply are not aware. Caroline did not say to herself, "I must not be jealous of Mummy because she has Daddy all to herself. I must not be jealous of Daddy because he has Mummy all to himself." No. But her behaviour showed that she was making an effort not to be overwhelmed by jealous and envious feelings.

It can be important to support and back up that aspect of a child's character which wants the parents to have something of a life of their own. In one family rather too much teasing of a small boy went on. From early days John and Maria Coleman – a very young couple – had noticed that Mark didn't like it when they kissed each other and hugged. Mark would protest loudly and try to separate them. They found it rather funny, as anyone might. But Mark's father began to use it to tease Mark; he would deliberately put his arm around Mark's mother and say, "She's all mine!" It was rather like over-exciting a puppy. And just as a teased puppy gets angry and uncertain-tempered, Mark began to become even less tolerant of his parents' togetherness and to be confirmed in his idea that it was something deliberately engineered to make him feel left out and angry. This was unhelpful, as all children (indeed, all people) have contrary concepts in their heads: on one hand there is the notion of strong, reliable, kind parents who join together in a friendly way to promote the happiness of their children. On the other hand there is an idea of big bad people, who get together for nasty purposes.

The final point about a four-year-old's feelings towards his or her parents is that they are markedly mixed. For some time now the child has been trying to get to grips with the idea that you can both love and hate the same person. The person whom you think is a bore and a nuisance, who keeps on intruding into your lovely imaginings about having mummy all to yourself for ever – that person is the same person as the daddy you admire and adore with all your heart. Or perhaps you have on another occasion all sorts of pleasant ideas of how you and Daddy will get together and have a wonderful exciting time, free from nagging old Mummy and that awful baby she seems to like so much – and then, of course, you have to see that old witch "nagger-knickers" is also the Mummy whom you love and think so brilliant and beautiful.

Only children

Your four-year-old may be an only child. Siblings may be born in the future, or indeed they may not. What are some of the thinking points about only children?

People are inclined to point out the disadvantages of being an only child, so that the parents of a singleton can feel quite guilty. We hear people muttering dire warnings: the only child will be selfish, unable to share, self-centred and spoilt. Well, the only child has no monopoly of these undesirable qualities. Of course, to be one child with all the attention of two parents, or one parent, is a different experience from being one of three or four. But if there has been a feeling of shortage in the family, or if there have been unresolved rivalries between brothers and sisters then a child can grow up in a large family and be very much unable to share in a truly generous spirit. On the whole it is perfectly possible to develop into a person who has brotherly or sisterly relationships with other people even if one doesn't have brothers and sisters of one's own.

Most parents of only children are sensibly aware that cousins, next-door-neighbours and nursery friends are essential additions to the life of an only child. Much depends on the sort of parenting that is offered. It seems to me that something which can make a good deal of difference to the parent's attitude towards having a single child is the question of whether that parent has in some way managed to think about all the children that he or she *hasn't* had. Most people are at some point sad when their family is complete, whether it's complete after one or after many. We may be thoroughly relieved on balance – no more nappies, no more broken nights – but just occasionally most people have a flash of sadness about something gone for good or about children who will never be. I think it is particularly important for the only child to have the idea that in *some* ways his parents might have liked more children, or at least that they have room in their imagination for others. Whether a family is limited to one because of practical constraints – scarce resources, demanding careers – or because other children simply didn't happen, it can be reassuring for a child to realise that his parents didn't stop at one just because he was such a trial.

This is something to bear in mind as a child grows: it hardly applies to a four-year-old, because most people haven't really decided whether a four-year-old will be an only child or not. It may be different when the parent is on his or her own with the child. Here, as with the child of any age with a single parent, some thinking needs to be done about a relationship which can become exclusive without either parent or child quite realising it.

Brothers and sisters

What position in the family does your four-year-old have? Is he the youngest, the eldest, or in the middle? The fact may have a lot of bearing upon his development and his relationship with his brothers and sisters.

Many four-year-olds do have a sibling, because plenty of parents don't want to leave too big a gap between babies. Let us first think of the four-year-old who is the first child, the elder of two or perhaps the eldest of three already. He or she will have been asked to give up the position of baby quite thoroughly by now and probably will be thought of by the parents as a big capable person. Sometimes it is hard to feel that you as a parent have not one but two or three babies with conflicting demands on your hands, but most parents realise that with several small children like this, all must have a turn at being babied sometimes.

When this can't happen, it is too much of a strain on the four-year-old. The Pipersons were a sad little family. Katy, Susan and Tony were aged four, two and one. Their young mother, not much past childhood herself, had had a deprived life and was struggling to bring them up without the support of anyone else. What was striking to people who came in to try to help was that Katy had identified herself with all that was motherly in her mother and was trying to look after the two younger ones. But when Susan had a toy saucepan full of plasticene that Katy wanted, all Katy's feelings of being a deprived and desperate baby surfaced. She grabbed the saucepan, tore it out of Susan's grasp, hit Susan, bit her and made off. Here we see that the two parts of Katy simply did not join up. A thin, brittle grown-up part of her was in no way strong enough to restrain the urgent, greedy impulse which came from a baby aspect of her that was convinced it must scratch and grab or never get what it wanted. This is an extreme example, taken from a family in dire straits. It shows how far too much had been asked of Katy and how resentful and neglected she felt. But even in more fortunate and ordinary families something like this can happen.

When a four-year-old is expecting a sibling for the first time, he or she will have had a good long go of being the small one and often be quite ready to move on. However, it is as well to be prepared for the unexpected. Sometimes the most self-possessed children can be taken unawares by feelings of rivalry and loneliness. Rosemary's mother and father thought she was quite old enough to go and stay with a fond aunt while her mother was in hospital having the new baby; her mother quite fancied what she thought would be a rest. But after Rosemary had heard that she had a new brother she grew more and more restless. Visiting her mother and the baby, she wept. Her aunt got very worried as Rosemary couldn't go to sleep and didn't want to eat. Next day the grown ups decided on a complete change of plan. Rosemary went home to Daddy, and Mother came home with baby early. Rosemary was much reassured by the prompt way in which people had realised how upset she was and had taken action. It was as though the grown-ups had conveyed to her by their actions a message like, "We made a mistake. We're sorry."

The four-year-old who comes somewhere in the middle of a family will be launched already on the exploration of what all the different relationships mean, and mean in terms of laying a foundation for all future ones. There is probably not much that a small book can tell parents in the thick of it about the hurly-burly of sibling relationships. Sometimes the one in the middle will yearn to join the older ones; sometimes it will be a comfort to relax and be the big one to the younger set. In general, though, this applies no more to the four-year-old than to any other child, it does seem worth remarking that usually, whatever the quarrelling and the problems, children in a family seem to swap round and take turns to be the easiest or the most difficult. Conversely, if a pattern is too fixed and permanent, this may be something which needs attention. In a family of two boys, Dan was four years the elder. He seemed stuck with the character of "difficult but clever", having from birth been demanding, not a great sleeper, choosy, but ambitious and forward. James was by contrast a wonderfully easy baby. His mother said, "The sun shines out of him." He continued relaxed and admired. The boys did not get on. Dan felt James was preferred. However, what nobody realised till much later was that James secretly felt Dan was the lucky one! Clever Dan, reading, playing football in the team, was greatly admired and envied by James who felt he could never hope to emulate him and fell back on the easy charm. This didn't alter until James stopped being a baby at home and entered the world of nursery and then school. James found that it was bearable to be a cross and frustrated person some of the time. Dan stopped feeling that he was the only nasty one, and also both boys were relieved of the worrying notion that Dan had got all the brains, as James developed his own abilities and skills. Dan cheered up and their relationship improved.

This touches on the last point I want to make, which involves thinking about the four-year-old who is the baby in the family. James was the baby of two, but some are the end of a long line, especially if there are step- children involved. All last children have in common the fact that they have never been ousted. The nice aspects of this are obvious; less obvious, perhaps, is the fact that nobody has come along behind them and given them a push up the ladder. So the baby of the family, who can seem very young indeed still at the age of four in contrast to how an eldest seems at four, sometimes needs some thought and help to establish his or her independence.

Expanding horizons

The four-year-old is often already at nursery or play-group. As I said earlier, the principal relationship, the one round which others revolve, is probably with the grown-up in charge. That is not to say that the friendship, companionship and sense of membership of a group which nursery can bring are less important. However, the child who gets the best from nursery is the child who has a solid base of trust in friendly adults. Children in a nursery group will probably have some sort of feeling at the back of their minds like "We're all Miss Fowler's children" (or "Janet's children", or however the leader or teacher is called). As such, they are brothers and sisters to each other and nursery is an expansion of the family. Hence it is important for the group to be one where every child can be borne in mind by an adult, and where each child's strengths and weaknesses, likes and dislikes, needs and wishes can be remembered. Four is a good age for moving beyond the immediate family, as children often spontaneously show by asking to visit a relative, go next door to play and so on. What used quite often to be for our needs and convenience just as much as theirs turns from something they can manage to cope with into a positive pleasure for them.

Single parents

I am very conscious that I have written a good deal about parents and that not every child is brought up in a household with both a mother and a father. Human beings are ingenious and resourceful and there are many different ways of doing things. However, we have to think what is variable and what is invariable. Children have been brought up in all sorts of different settings; we are preoccupied now with one-parent families created by choice or by separation or divorce, but death saw to it in past centuries that many children were motherless or fatherless, members of reconstituted families or orphans brought up by adoptive parents. Think of all the maiden aunts who adopted bereaved children. The family setting is variable.

What is invariable is the way in which a child has an inevitable desire to know about mothers and fathers in general, and his or her own mother and father in particular. The question, "Where do babies come from?" and its companion, "Where did I come from?" are questions on the minds of four-year-olds. The matter of fathers and mothers in general is catered for in all sorts of ways. Children meet and get to know all sorts of people of both sexes, either friends of their parents or parents of their friends; neighbours, people in shops, people on the television and in books all are digested and processed in the child's mind and add to the ideas they form of men and women and the relation between them.

As for the particular question of your *own* mother and father, it is a burning one for every child. The infant in the mother's arms is taking in her mental qualities – her attentiveness, her affection, her thinking mind. He progresses to a strong interest in her thoughts and ideas; he wants to know all about her and to be acquainted with her knowledge, memories and opinions. He wants to know her. Now, if his father, shall we say, is not there to be known, at very least he wants to know *about* him. What really can be a problem is when the absent parent is disliked or regarded with very mixed feelings by the parent in charge. It is one thing if relations between parents are reasonably amiable and the child can find out about the absent parent through letters, telephone calls, visits and longer stays. Then he or she can discover the parent for himself or herself. More difficult by far is the unseen, unknown parent who only lives in the mind of the remaining one. If the lost parent is dead, then there is in a way less difficulty. Enid, now long grown up, was a little girl whose father was killed in the war. She recalled all sorts of sadness and difficulty but she also was brought up with a strong impression that her parents had loved each other, that her father had valued and admired her mother and she him. Her father lived on in her mother's mind as someone who would never have left them both if he had not been so unkindly taken.

If the absent parent lives on as something very different from this, the matter needs care and thought. For a child will want to know about his or her father, and it may be important to salvage some picture which is not utterly coloured by bitterness and distaste. A child can over the years gain some understanding of someone who was mistaken, unfortunate or ill. But it is harder to accommodate the idea that you are the child of somebody cruel and bad. These matters are ones to be thought about over a long time. But it is at this age that they often crop up in the form of questions which cannot be ignored.

CHAPTER TWO

KEEPING THE CHILD SAFE: THE NEED FOR GROWN-UPS

Framework and structures

The four-year-old's growing independence of mind can only flourish within a secure framework. Too much doubt and unsureness, too many unexpected and bewildering happenings overload the mental system of a small child. Thus we find that he or she positively relishes a routine – not a rigid crushing routine where there is no space for change and experiment and nice surprises – but the sort of routine which provides a structure within which there can be freedom of movement.

He or she is gradually learning to use the structures we all use, the pattern of each day, the week and the week-end, the passing seasons, the yearly celebrations like birthdays and Christmas. Most parents intuitively realise that it helps a child to make sense of new experiences if these patterns can be used. A four-year-old, Georgina, on a five-day visit to a household she did not know well, was greatly reassured by her hostess, who had made her a calendar. It was labelled from Friday to Tuesday; Georgina was to tick a day off each evening at bedtime. Special events were marked: Saturday said "Zoo", Sunday said "Tea at Sophie's house" and Tuesday said in large letters "Mummy and Daddy come at tea-time". Following this through and discussing it enabled Georgina to get a hold on things.

Georgina, it was reported, seemed to have liked this idea of planning ahead. Soon after this she left playgroup and started in the nursery class of an infant school. Her mother took her on a visit and the shape of the day was explained to them; making and doing things first, then a drink and play outside . . . Georgina listened seriously and watched the children. During the days that followed she told her mother several times, "First I shall do some beads and sticking," or, "First I shall play in the home corner." She was dealing with her natural nervousness by thinking ahead. You could also say that she had learnt from the experience of her visit away from home that giving something a shape and talking it over can be a help.

Rules

What is allowed and what is not allowed will vary from family to family. On the one hand there are the inessentials, the smaller rules. One mother will feel really unhappy if she hasn't got at least part of the home kept for the grown-ups, and she will want toys and other children's clutter kept out of the sitting room. That will be her way of protecting a space for herself, her partner and her friends. Another mother might find this unnecessary, silly, impossible or all three – and yet be surprisingly firm about her own rules. Each family has its rules, spoken and unspoken. First there is the smaller sort ("no gumboots in the hall") about which there will be a lot of variation. What these rules have in common is an attempt to make things fairer and more comfortable for people who live in a household: the disagreement is about how this may be achieved. Even families who say they haven't got any rules find on examination that they *have*. Then there is a more important set of rules; rules about how people in general ought to behave. Again, there may be disagreement about relative importance of rules (how unallowable is spitting?) or how to enforce and administer them (how do you see that big children don't bully little ones?) but we mostly agree that cruelty, exploitation, lying and stealing (for instance) are not acceptable.

Four-year-olds are becoming interested in rules, both in the sense of what you're allowed to do and what you aren't, and also in the wider sense of what is right and what is not. Sometimes they can be very hard on themselves. "Am I allowed to go on the balcony?" asked Jemima: and "Am I allowed to walk on the grass?" Since her mother had never mentioned either matter, let alone said that you were or weren't allowed to do it, her mother was quite upset. She felt that it was her fault that Jemima was seeing the world as a place of strict and petty rules. Since she wished to be relaxed and easy with Jemima, her mother felt puzzled and anxious. Now, funnily enough, puzzled and anxious is exactly what Jemima was feeling as she tried to sort out what she might do and what she might not. So she conveyed by a roundabout route her emotions to her mother. And in a roundabout way, her mother dealt with the puzzlement and anxiety by explaining patiently about balconies and grass. The small child's conscience can be much stricter than we would like: indeed, you could say that a very fierce and punitive approach to rule-breaking is an infantile thing.

Guidelines

Four-year-olds are becoming interested, as I have just said above, in right and wrong, good and bad. In short, morality concerns them. However, our complex and subtle adult approach is likely to be too much for them; they still need a kind, clear approach which doesn't confuse them. They need plain distinctions between good and bad which later they can modify and query.

Nicholas was keen on playing soldiers. His parents were concerned that he shouldn't get carried away by idealising a rough, brutal approach to life, a picture of the world where the most ruthless wins. However, as they observed him play they realised that he was trying to sort out an idea of a "good soldier", of somebody who defends what he values with courage and vigour. Children need to distinguish between the strength and power of a bully, and the strength which has nothing to do with bullying and everything to do with firmness and determination.

They need the concept of a "good policeman" no matter how hard that concept may be to bring to life in our adult world. It is noticeable that in lots of children's games – the "cops and robbers" of years ago, the Skeletor and He-Man or the Teenage Turtles of more recent times, the goodies and the baddies get a bit blurred. Both sides seem in danger of behaving rather alike. In view of this, it is important that we do try to keep alive in our approach the notion of a kind, firm, just person in charge, a person who wants to see fair play and won't let bullies thrive.

Limits and boundaries

Four-year-olds need people who make the limits clear, who just won't allow them to behave in an extreme way and who don't see them as too powerful.

Simon was at the park playground sitting on a see-saw. His mother wanted to go. He yelled and screamed and protested, kicking and lashing. His mother said, rather breathlessly, "O.K. I suppose we can stay a bit," and replaced him. A few minutes later she tried once more. The same scene repeated itself. Later still two other young mothers watched as Simon's mother alternately placated him with coaxing and tried to carry him to his buggy. "I think she's a bit frightened of him," said one watcher to the other.

What does this rather too tentative treatment make Simon feel like? Presumably he feels all-powerful. He can over-ride not only his mother's wishes, but also her sensible adult self who is thinking sensible adult thoughts like, "It's time for tea," or "It's going to rain." So Simon keeps on triumphing over his mother. For a bit he is pleased; he's won; he's got what he wants: but after that? He doesn't seem to be enjoying himself much. Presumably he is feeling unsure and unsafe. Simon has some idea that he is only small. He also has some idea that he needs looking after. If the big people in his life are to be under his control, behaving as though they can be bullied, who will be the people to take charge, and take care of him?

How can a child learn to set his own limits? Only with the help of grown-ups who are not overwhelmed by the uncompromising quality of childish rage. Boundaries must be drawn, or any child grows anxious. Simon wouldn't have understood the word "guilt", but guilty is what he felt as he bullied his mother and made her look silly.

Limits are necessary in all sorts of ways, and the successful setting of them is a relief to a child. Diana at four was still carting a bottle of milk around. Calling it her "Big Bottle" in a possessive way, she would suck from it in a half-defiant fashion, as though she knew very well she had outgrown it and didn't need it; but she made no movement whatsoever to stop. Her parents believed she should really give it up of her own accord, so apart from a few hints they had let her carry on, thinking she needed it for security reasons. However, nursery school was looming. Diana was a large, well-built girl and looked pretty foolish with a bottle hanging from her teeth. During the holidays before she started full-day nursery, her parents conferred together. The upshot was that, bracing herself, Diana's mother put the bottle away. When Diana demanded it, her mother said, "It's gone, Diana. I'm going to throw it away. You don't need it any more." And to he mother's long-lasting surprise, Diana replied, "All right, Mummy," and went to watch telly without it. She never demanded it again and in a few days spoke of "When I used to have a bottle," as though it were years ago. It was as if she had been waiting for this to happen and couldn't think why it hadn't happened before. Diana sensed the absolute decision her parents had made, and probably the relief resided in her feeling they had joined together to curb something which she had outgrown and wasn't doing her much good.

Punishment and smacking

Small children can make us feel primitive; they can be most irritating and can call out in us a wish to retaliate and to punish. It seems useful to distinguish between this (a rather ignoble if powerful wish to get one's own back on this awful child) and the use of warnings and sanctions. Warnings are a little different from threats. Ralph and Nicholas were playing with a water pistol. They were getting wild and shooting it all around, including over the dry washing on the line. "If you wet that washing again I shall have to put the guns away for today," said his father. "You're getting too excited." The two boys just couldn't control themselves, and the guns were taken away.

This is very different from another occasion when the boys somehow maddened their father by absolutely refusing to calm down. Instead of being able to stay calm and firm, he got really rattled. They got under his skin. He started to lose his temper instead of just speaking severely. He yelled at them to shut up and get inside, and he followed this up with a cuff each. Later he felt deflated and sorry, as though he had himself lost adult status and behaved like a big brother rather than a father.

With regard to smacking children, we are in a difficult position today. Probably most people would agree in a general way that it is better not to hit children. Some people hold strongly to the view that it is not only unnecessary but wrong; others are not so sure. What we can say is that times have changed. A hundred years ago, even fifty years ago, the general opinion was quite different; smacking small children and caning older ones was not considered abnormal. This has altered only gradually, so that today's parents – born twenty-five to forty years ago – were born into a different atmosphere. In short, most of us were smacked. When our children are naughty, our reason may tell us not to hit them while our instinct, dating back to our own childhood, may impel us to give them a wallop. So many parents feel torn and guilty about this, and indeed it is undeniable that if we really do lose our tempers, as Ralph and Nicholas's father did, we feel that we have broken a boundary, "gone over the top".

CHAPTER THREE

WORK AND PLAY

Explorations

Work are play are close together for a four-year-old; indeed, you could say that play is the four-year-old's job, serious and meaningful as it can be. The four-year-old is exploring not only the outer world of people and things, and the less tangible world of ideas beyond himself, but also the inner world of his own thoughts and emotions. He or she wishes to puzzle away at questions and his or her thirst for knowledge is frank.

For the first time, the great questions of human existence begin to come into his mind. Where do we come from? where do we go to? how do things work? Life and death, religion, sexuality are all matters which concern the child at this particularly fertile time when he or she is no longer a baby, and before the schoolboy or schoolgirl years arrive with their more practical, less philosophical flavour. Many parents are surprised by how closely their small children think about God, or death, or sex, and what deep matters they approach.

With some of these, it can be a delicate matter to know how to respond. For example, children often want to know where babies come from. It seems extremely important with any question to be straightforward and truthful, because a child's trust can be easily bruised. Four year olds can be made to feel small and humiliated, let alone bewildered and misled by evasive or even untruthful answers to questions of fact. Their investigations may either continue independent of adults, perhaps despising them, or they may think that these questions are too alarming to be faced directly and nervously give up on thinking about them.

But it can be important to remember that a child is not necessarily asking you to tell him every single thing you know about sex. There is such a thing as a too high dosage of information. Children need their replies to be graded in relation to how much they are asking for and how much they can digest. Questions about the death of a relative, for instance, also need to be answered with absolute truth; but we would want to offer some protection to a small child and not give them distressing and frightening details.

The other thing, of course, is that you have to realise that a child's imagination will sometimes prevail over all the factual information that you can possibly give. Jessica, aged six, and Jane, aged four, were riding with their mother in the back of a taxi after a most exhausting day when Jessica piped up, "Mummy, Jane says babies come out of tummy buttons. Tell her, Mummy, they don't." So Mummy pulled herself together and did what she thought was a rather good job of explaining about babies in tummies and how they got there and how they grew and came out of a special hole. Unfortunately, she was flabbergasted to hear Jane say a few days later, "Babies *really* come out of tummy buttons, don't they?" Jane's mother instantly felt that Jane was wrestling with the answer she had been given in the taxi and finding it rather hard to swallow. So she just said, "No, darling, not really," and left it at that, not forcing the truth upon Jane, though not agreeing with her fantasy either.

Doing and making, helping and mending

Small children are learning all the time. One of the attractive things about them is the fact that things we take for granted are fresh to them and a source of continuous interest. A bus ride, a train journey, a visit to a launderette, going to feed the ducks, cleaning the bathroom, can all come under detailed scrutiny. Helping the play leader at playgroup, making things out of egg boxes and cornflake packets, watching workmen mending the road; all these things harmonise with a four-year-old's deep and abiding interest in how things work and are made. Children of this age are creative – not creative in the grown-up way, but full of imagination and liveliness.

Not only are they discovering how the world works and what their own and other people's skills and capacity are; they are learning about something else essential, about how people constantly dip into their resources of hopefulness and make new things, mend what is broken, put right things that have gone wrong, try out ideas, clean up dirty places. Children need the experience of making and doing things, not only to learn about how things are made and done but because it makes them feel capable and good.

Four-year-olds are sorting out the difference between the world of the imagination and the world of reality in many different ways. One way is by finding out what really happens as distinct from what you wish would happen or what you fear might happen.

Nursery school or group

Many four-year-olds, perhaps most, spend part of their week in the company of children of their own age and away from home. When the group is stable and kindly and imaginatively run, the advantages are obvious; under the eye and protection of the grown-ups the children can not only learn about each other, but also learn to share people and things, and learn to do things together. A parent would be hard put to keep going every day with all the activities which a nursery group can provide; the painting and the cutting out, the growing of plants or the baking of buns, the singing and the stories and the co-operative games.

It is a great pity if formal learning at this age starts to take over from the easy informality of good nursery education. In this country there has been much controversy and anxiety over education, with plenty of people feeling concerned that things have become too free and easy and that children neither learn to persevere with difficulties nor acquire some of the skills that only come with discipline. However, these anxieties have little or no place when we are thinking about nursery education. The child who is persevering, and helped to persevere, with a jigsaw or a drawing or with trying to make friends is learning self-discipline and practising concentration.

There are dangers in pressing children to struggle away with reading and writing at the age of four. One danger is that work and play may become too split apart, with the possibility that work will start to seem boring and play delightful but somehow a waste of time. Another danger is that a young child should prematurely taste the problems of failure. Of course, we all need determination in the face of reverses. But the four-year-old needs to practise this in a spontaneous way and to be helped informally with it, rather than to be drilled and to feel that work is a hard and humiliating thing.

That is not to say that those with a taste for it should be discouraged. There are children who long to be able to read, and learn easily, just as there are those who do drawing after drawing, or those who show an obvious natural talent for football. It seems important to be flexible. Children vary within the same family. In one family, the parents didn't teach the eldest to read, believing it was better done by experts. He went to school and learnt to read at once. The next boy, treated similarly, didn't learn to read till he was over seven. His parents thought this was a bit late so his mother taught the next child, a girl, to read before she went to school. This was a great success. However, when she tried to teach the youngest girl at a similar age, they both found it such uphill work that they left it for school – and that girl learnt perfectly well a year later.

Being too grown up

Perhaps one can ask if there is such a thing as being too grown up. Or, alternatively, what do I mean by this as related to a four-year-old? Of course there is such a thing as a four-year-old who is well able to manage what is asked of him or her; a girl or boy who is active in body and mind and enjoys pressing on with the business of growing up. This doesn't mean that a lively, cheerful child should experience no fits of babyishness, no crying and unreasonableness, no lapses into timidity or defiance. In keeping with what was said earlier about the vulnerability and dependence of a four-year-old, and the continuing need for a good deal of adult attention, we have to remember that a four-year-old is quite a baby still. He needs emotional help to just the same degree as he needs practical help. To return to the notion of being "too grown up", we can sometimes see a child who is so apparently competent that too much can be asked of him or her. Terry was a four-year-old from a family where the children had to do quite a lot of looking after themselves. He was big and strong and thought nothing of going to the shops alone or to the park with his brother and no adult. He tended to be lordly and rough at nursery. "He's no shrinking violet," said one mother to another, sounding half-annoyed and alarmed for her own child whom she might have been thinking of as a more delicate flower. But the teachers soon saw that inside the large blustery exterior there was a very little Terry, who was frightened of not getting enough and of being trampled down. The little Terry sheltered under the protection of the rough outward Terry. It was the teachers' job to help him trust them and their grown-up capacity to see that the rule for all the children was "fair do's and no bullying", and to see that if he were to relinquish the character of a big boy who doesn't need help, he would still be quite safe. This was, of course, easily the most important aspect of the work of the nursery class for Terry. He learnt to relax into being a little boy, and hence into being much more teachable and friendly.

The most mature and the least mature aspects of our four-year-old both need attention. Jessica was very forward with many things; as an elder sister she had pressed on ambitiously with learning how to do things at four that most of her companions could not. She was clever and determined and got admiration and praise. However, in her as in Terry the teachers could see a less sure side, a side which was bossy and competitive, and which sometimes found it hard to play comfortably with other children. When Jessica's parents talked to the teachers they all recognised that even though Jessica could read like a six-year-old and do up her shoe-laces like a six-year-old, she was four-years-old at heart, and sometimes even less, and had plenty to learn about how to manage her feelings in relation to other children.

Growing up through play

Much of a four-year-old's growing up is done through imaginative play, through all kinds of pretending and make-believe. For instance, once Jessica had settled down at nursery school, she went through a period both at home and at school of playing quite intensely by herself with a family of dolls. She was using her play as a way of thinking about how people get on together. She made up stories to herself about the dolls. Sometimes she was absolutely in charge and the dolls did exactly what she wanted, but at other times they didn't behave so nicely, and rows and quarrels broke out.

Another form of make-believe is pretending to be somebody else. Whether by actually dressing up, or pretending to dress up, four-year-olds feel a need to explore different characters and to develop the way in which they identify with other people. For example, it is no accident that playing fathers and mothers is so popular. Children are deeply occupied with thinking "What does it mean to be a girl? What does it mean to be a boy?" The answers will partly depend on the society where they live, the ideas about girls and boys and women and men that are current. But they will also depend on the way in which two things combine: first, the safe feeling that you are what and who you are, and second, your capacity for an endless number of different identifications. In imagination we can have knowledge of what it is like to be all sorts of people beyond our immediate selves. This is linked with knowing and being in touch with different aspects of our own characters. The little boy who is rough and scornful in his dealings with even smaller children is out of touch with his own capacity to be protective and gentle. The little girl who hovers timidly round the edges and daren't join in is out of touch with something more enterprising and courageous in herself.

Sometimes parents are concerned about the identifications which their children seem to be forming. A mother decided in her own views about the need for girls to be vigorous and wary of the idea of sexual stereotyping became puzzled when her daughter developed a passion for necklaces and frills and the character of a little princess. The more she tried to press Nell to wear jeans and to express a view that jewellery and ballet dancing are soppy, the more Nell dug in her heels and tried to array herself like the Queen of Sheba. It is useful to be aware that such passions as Nell's are usually temporary. Nell was indeed exploring her wish to be a grand, dressed-up lady, and the more her mother was felt to pour cold water on it, the more Nell felt cross and threatened. Similarly, Mike's father got angry and uncomfortable when he saw Mike all dressed up in a long frock and carrying a handbag. But Mike was not really confused. He knew he was a boy. However, at that time he was thinking what it might be like to be a mum, and he expressed it dramatically.

At this age children usually switch around quite readily in their games. The time perhaps to ask oneself questions and to think about it a bit more is if a child seems to get stuck with just one character for a long time. The child, for example, who is always taking the role of the baby in other children's games may be having some problems with asserting something more grown-up in herself. Terry, whom I mentioned earlier in the chapter, constantly claimed to be Superman. All the other little boys sometimes liked being Superman, but Terry clung to the idea with a tenacity which showed that he wasn't just toying with the exciting idea of being magic and invulnerable. He was trying to believe that it was true, because underneath he felt fragile and unsure.

Language and thought

Stories and drawings, music, poems and songs all appeal to children at this age. If one looks closely at rhymes and tales that have stood the test of time – let alone the very excellent new ones which keep coming out – one can see how they address children's preoccupations and perform a function by giving these preoccupations a shape and a form in which they can be thought about. Nursery rhymes have often lasted for centuries. They must have answered a need, or they would have been forgotten. The "little girl who had a little curl" about whom it is said,

"When she was good, she was very very good

But when she was bad, she was horrid!''
addresses a child's need to come to grips with the fact that he or
she is not always nice; and the fact that this problem (of being
both "good" and "horrid") is universal. The Knave of Hearts
who stole the tarts was known to Alice in Wonderland in 1865,
and he still today stands for all children's naughty wishes to grab
things that aren't theirs and make off with them. Humpty
Dumpty's pride goes before a fall; he is like the child who gets
wildly over-excited and comes a bit of a cropper.

More complicated are some children's books, the best of
which are true literature. Beatrix Potter's books, for instance,
stretch a child's thinking capacity as well as engaging his
fascinated wishes. "The Tale of Peter Rabbit" caters both for
that part of a small child which wants to be law- abiding and to
identify with Flopsy, Mopsy and Cottontail, "who were good
little bunnies", and also that part of the same girl or boy which
wants to be like Peter, who "ran straight away to Mr
McGregor's garden" (where he had expressly been told not to
go) "and squeezed under the gate". It is a story about what you
do when Mummy's back is turned, about what to do with your
independence. But it is told in such a way as to be sympathetic
with Peter's adventurousness and his mistakes and it opens the
way to a thoughtful rather than a rigid view of right and wrong.
A child with a limited opportunity to learn new words is limited
in his thinking too, and acquaintance with books can, as people
often say, open new worlds.

Pictures and songs come into the same category. The
child who responds to music or who observes pictures and
draws is developing ways of thinking as well as laying a
foundation for a possible future love of these things.

Movement and activity

Nobody needs me to tell them that four-year-olds love running about, climbing, having a go at bicycles (with stabilisers at first), and all sorts of physical activity. It is obvious that they enjoy an increasing mastery of their bodies. The only parents who may be bothered are the ones with children at the extreme ends of the spectrum; children who are clearly timid or those who are reckless. If your child is one of the timid ones, a common-sense approach is probably best. That is to say, it is important to remember that if your child is four he has plenty of time to change and develop. Rosemary was afraid of the water in the summer she was four. Her mother got caught up with Rosemary's anxiety and started to think Rosemary was embarking on a lifelong dread of swimming. However, as it became clear that persuasion only made Rosemary worse, the parents decided to let well alone for the time being, and not to press it. The summer after, Rosemary went into the pool with the bravest.

The other end of the line is represented by those children who don't just betray an aptitude for climbing and running but who seem to want to deny all fear and climb too high and too dangerously, or who want to spend all their time in physical activity and never sitting quietly. Again, common sense tells us that the grown-ups mustn't get carried away too and deny the danger. Also, that children do need times when they are being quietly attended to, and that over-activity and over-excitement can mask some more vulnerable feelings which need attention.

Television

Small children love the programmes specially designed for them and often form quite a bond with them; "we've got to get home for 'Sesame Street' ", for example. However, although most parents use the television as a kind of nanny sometimes, knowing that children will sit still and not bother while it's on, most parents are also aware that a machine is not a real substitute for a person. Television is even different from looking at a book. If you look at pictures in a book you go at your own speed. You put something into it. You can go forward or back to look at something again. You can read the book you fancy. Television programmes wait for nobody. Children sometimes use videos as books, running and re-running them and making them their own, thinking about them and being the various characters. We have to remember that films and television have a powerful capacity to take us out of ourselves, however, and a small child with a sense of self not fully developed can get taken over and overwhelmed by too much of them. And there is such a thing as children being alarmed and over-stimulated by grown-up programmes or programmes that are too strong for them, which is why parents like to keep a close eye on what children watch. Even programmes which are not obviously unsuitable can sometimes be upsetting. Sara was watching Children's Television when she became terribly upset and frightened by the picture of an unhappy sea-bird covered in oil. Her father was glad he was there to receive her distress promptly and to do his best to explain and comfort.

Toys and playing

People don't need me to tell them that nowadays a great

number of different sorts of toys are available for your four-year-old. We are trying in this little book to think about the meaning of things to the child, and of course all the different toys will have different meanings. We have already in passing thought about constructional toys, which help a child to think about how things work, how things are made, how things are repaired. We have looked briefly at physical activity; and we can see how mastery of a climbing frame, a bike, a pedal-tractor can healthily develop mental confidence as well as bodily muscle. There are toys like dolls and teddy bears which can acquire personality; we only have to remember Winnie-the-Pooh with his simplicity and boastfulness, or his friend the donkey Eeyore with his dreadful gloomy pessimism!

Play involves thinking about the two basic realities: the reality of the outside world, of places and things and the people who inhabit it; and the reality of the inside world – the world of the imagination, of memory, ideas and feelings, a world which is populated with characters just as surely as the outside world is filled with actual people. In the four-year-old's play he or she is working out essential questions about the nature of reality. What are the differences between "real life" and "pretend"? between fact and fiction? truth and lies? lies and make-believe?

Parents are sometimes welcome to join in, even dragged along to be participants. Occasionally this becomes too much. Children who really can't play alone are a bit of a worry as well as a nuisance. Most children over time display a capacity to play with adults, with children, and by themselves. Individuals have preferences, of course, but on the whole we can usually see all three categories represented. If a child is for any length of time timid and unsure about playing, the parents often have to bend their minds to understanding why.

Carola's mother sought professional advice about what was the matter with Carola. She seemed so nervous and diffident about playing – almost as if frightened of her toys. The child psychotherapist watched Carola with her mother. There were dolls and toys in the room. Carola started to play a little as her mother talked: she took a doll and tentatively began to put it in the cot. As she did so, the doll bumped against the side. "Oh, poor doll!" cried her mother in a loud and anxious tone. Carola shrank. She retreated near her mother, dropping the doll. Gradually it became clear that while some children relish enthusiastic joining-in from adults, Carola was one of those who need plenty of assurance that there is a clear line between fact and fantasy. Dolls are dolls, and people are people. There used to be an Andy Pandy book that finished up the story by saying, "Bears are bears, and prickly hedgehogs are prickly hedgehogs." Carola came to enjoy this book very much. She needed to feel firmly that things are what they are. Also, her worries had got into her mother, and her mother had got so anxious that she was returning the worries to Carola instead of being able to mull things over and see what was the matter. Once again, the presence of a third person to consult proved rather helpful.

What about how many and what sort of toys to get? Everyone likes to buy a child a toy. We often – and why not? – like to buy children things we didn't have ourselves, or things which pleased us in our childhood. Sometimes, of course, our children are different from us; sometimes we unexpectedly get it wrong. Also, many parents have ruefully observed expensive toys gathering dust while the four-year-old occupies herself with a little old saucepan, two plastic beakers, some empty fish-paste jars and a lot of mud. At the risk of sounding a bore, I would think that common-sense dictates a middle line, a line which sometimes follows a child's interests, sometimes introduces new ones; a line which keeps a balance between too little and too much.

Too many toys can pose problems. It is probably true that if a child feels that new things can be bought all the time it is harder to invest interest and meaning in what is there. Lots of broken toys strewn around make a depressing sight, even if they only form a background for the newest ones. Without wanting to be too moralistic, we probably all would rather our children did not feel that the way to happiness is by having more and more *things*. The child who says, "I want, I want" all the time isn't satisfied by getting more and more. He or she is trying to convey that something is missing, or feels as if it's missing. And that feeling will only be quietened briefly by a new toy or a packet or sweets. It's more important to look around and see what's the matter than to lull the complaints with treats.

One last thought about toys. Four-year-olds are frequently still attracted to some beloved Teddy or perhaps to a blanket. It can be quite a sensitive matter to treat such an object respectfully, but from an adult perspective. On the one hand, we feel how important, meaningful and sometimes necessary these objects are to a four-year-old. On the other hand, it isn't always helpful to behave as if we really agreed that the world would disintegrate without Teddy. All children need the secure conviction that they are in the charge of grown-ups, people who have a mature grip on reality. Against this background they can safely play out conflicts and questions about the real and the not real.

CHAPTER FOUR

ANXIETY AND DISTRESS

Dealing with unhappiness

Four is a great age for anxieties. Surely most four-year-olds, even the sunniest, have the odd bad dream or some irrational fear, as well as all the ordinary ups and downs of daily life. We would all like our children to be happy. It can be hard to accept that it is not in our power to make them happy all the time. But we can perform a service for them, a service which is irreplaceable in their development. We can take their fears, their worries and their problems seriously and we can give them our attention. Sometimes all we can do is to be with them while they are unhappy or unwell and keep them company. We cannot always take away a pain or undo a bad experience. But at least, especially if a child is really upset, we can give our full attention. This means, of course, that we suffer some of their upset too at times, and it can be a delicate matter when we struggle to keep an adult perspective and not to be overwhelmed by a child's distress. There can be few parents who have not, for example, been made blindly furious by some tale of unfairness done to their child. And many of us have become over-anxious when a child is unwell, often because we pick up and respond to a child's alarm as well as experiencing our own.

The process whereby a child can convey distress to an understanding and receptive adult and be made to feel better is a most important one for the child's emotional development. As everyday experience tells us, "a trouble shared is a trouble halved". You cannot turn back the clock and make a child not have fallen over, and you cannot really abolish the fact that this gave him a nasty shock and a sore knee that will take time to mend. But you can understand how bad he feels, you can listen to his distress and you can absorb it. There will be times, of course, where the child is on his own. There will be times when grown-ups are busy or unsympathetic, or when they will deny or make light of his pain. But if he has enough experience of times when someone can bear his pain or worry with him, his own resources to bear distress will increase. He will feel as though he carries around in his memory and his imagination, consciously and unconsciously, helpful figures who will stand by him in his hour of need. This is how children themselves learn to be helpful and sympathetic.

Peter realised his mother was upset. His father was away and his tired mother had had to put up with a series of problems culminating in a broken washing-machine. He was very glad to see the man come to mend it and spent time watching the repair and asking what had gone wrong. When the machine was working again and the man had gone both Peter and his mother felt better and had a cup of tea. Later on Peter went to see the lady downstairs, an older person whom he liked very much. He clearly described the problem and its solution, telling her that instead of washing the clothes properly and sending all the dirt away, the machine had gone wrong. The dirty water had started coming back and making the clothes inside all mucky. Mummy had got cross and then she cried a bit. But the man came after lunch and made the machine better.

Here we have a little story that tells us something about Peter and his ideas of making things better. The washing machine usually took in dirty clothes and made them clean, just as Peter usually had the experience of his mother coping with all sorts of things and sorting them out nicely. He would usually go to her if he felt he was in some kind of mess and get himself all sorted out. But today both the machine and Mummy seemed to have gone wrong. Peter may have been concerned to see that instead of Mummy coping with and processing any problems (including Peter's) she had become cross and anxious. No wonder he was relieved when the repair-man came. Of course, it was significant that Peter's father was away. The repair man functioned as a kind of daddy-person who put things right, and Peter was confirmed in a comfortable feeling that grown-ups could back each other up and that his mother knew how to get help. He was relieved of the lurking suspicion that it was up to him to make Mummy feel better.

Thinking about anxieties

There is a limit to how helpful a little book like this can be in thinking about a specific worry you have about your child, who after all is unique and in a unique position. But before I try to consider some particular ways in which anxieties may present themselves – in sleep disturbances, in tantrums, or in hyperactivity for example – there may perhaps be a general rule about how to start thinking about a four-year-old's problem. That is, to do a survey of his or her life, and the family's life, and to see what is happening at present which might have an indirectly disturbing effect upon your child. If a grandparent is ill, if a new baby is in the offing, if you have moved house, if a job has been lost or if anything else has happened to disturb the equilibrium of the family, your four-year-old, like any small child, may be acting as a kind of barometer of distress. You can look and see the child's individual life in the round, if there is nothing wrong in the family at large. How does the disturbance fit in? How is life going at nursery? What, in short, is the worry?

For instance, the sensitive Sara mentioned in the last chapter who shook with fear when she saw an oil-drenched sea-bird on television, was clearly affected in general by the fact that her parents' marriage was going through a difficult time. This and other incidents led both parents to feel concern that she was being shaken by their disagreements and they managed to pull together to spare her some of their problems.

Separation anxieties

There can of course be all sorts of different reasons for a four-year-old's not wanting to let a parent go. It is silly to pretend that one can generalise about it. But what one can say is that for some reason the child feels that he or she needs a real parent there to defend against the feelings of nervousness, loneliness or whatever they may be that threaten to engulf him or her when the parent goes away. In general, as with any anxiety, patience and thought are the only tools we can bring.

It can be disconcerting when a child who has cheerfully separated from us time and again suddenly gets anxious. This happened to Luke. He had been going to a child-minder ever since he was six months old for part of every day. So it would seem that he was well and truly used to his mother's going to work. However, when he started nursery class just before he was four, he failed to settle easily. He clung to his mother and cried, even after she had spent quite a long time staying with him. After she left he didn't want to join in. It took a long time and many tears – and of course much heart-searching and worry for his mother – before he accepted nursery and entered into life there.

How can we think about this? First of all, there really was a big difference between Luke's being one of only two children at the child-minder's house, and one of a class at nursery. He was probably missing his child- minder and feeling that the younger child (still with her) was having her all to himself. It also seemed that he had managed to ignore his mother's absence in a way while he was with his child-minder. It was almost as if he hadn't really thought about it: he felt comfortable with Mum and similarly comfortable with Jackie. When he went to nursery it was as if he felt pitched out into a world of lots of other children – and lots of other ideas. For the first time he wondered where his mother went. Why did she go away? What did she do instead of being with him? The reality of her absence, and the fact that he suddenly understood that when she wasn't with him, she was with somebody else, seemed to hit Luke for six. All the feelings about Mummy's going away which he had never had before came in a rush. It was as though he had never truly felt separate before, and now he did. He had to go through an experience of wanting her to stay and not being able to make her do so, of missing her, and then gradually finding that she did come back and that he could manage without either Mum or his child-minder Jackie.

Sleep disturbances

Sleep disturbances are sometimes related to separation anxieties: they can, of course, occur at any age; but they are frequently connected with anxieties about managing alone. Night is the time above all when, if you wake up, you are aware of being by yourself. In the dark, even the presence of a sleeping sibling in the room cannot always allay anxiety.

Often it is thoughts about parents, who are together, which interfere with a child's turning over and going back to sleep. In the first chapter I spoke of the four-year-old's vital preoccupation with the parents as a couple, and at night-time this preoccupation can be sharpened.

Sleep disturbances can occur, as other disturbances do, as a result of a change in the family circumstances which puts some extra strain on a child.

When her mother went back to work part-time, Jane started to have problems falling asleep in the evening. It was as though she would have time with her mother then if she couldn't have it earlier. This interfered with the family's evenings. Jessica wouldn't stay in bed if Jane wasn't there, so they were both up and down and their parents had no evening whatsoever. Alarmingly enough, things got worse. Jane now started to wake in the night and come regularly into her parents' room. She got into bed with them. She had occasionally done this before, but not often, and then she had obviously come for comfort and had not disturbed them greatly. Now she got in between them; she kicked and rolled and prevented all peaceful sleeping. So sometimes her mother would get up and go into Jane's bed with her. Or Jessica would wake up and join them all. Then their father, muttering, would leave and go to sleep in the spare room. Everyone would be tired out in the morning. The parents got edgy and bickered about what to do. The whole family was thrown.

In a sense you could say that the whole family was thrown by the mother's return to work. Jane was expressing something that everyone felt. Everyone had mixed feelings about Mum working outside the home. Jane, Jessica and Dad were all a little bit put out that Mum was going elsewhere. Jane seemed to express her feelings of being left by refusing to be apart from her mother when her mother was in the house, and she also seemed to feel that the whole normal order of things – adults in their place, children in theirs – was disarranged.

Finally the parents discussed it and agreed that something must be done. They decided to let the two girls stay up later and to spend time very definitely attending to them in the evenings instead of trying to pack them off at the old early hour. Of course, even the later hour still left some adult time; it was nowhere near as late as Jane had lately been going to bed. This was explained to Jessica and Jane. They were told that a new routine was beginning and it was put into practice. Of course, it didn't work like magic. But slowly the feeling that the parents had got to grips with the problem increased; the night-time visits died away and the girls remained in bed once they had gone. The girls seemed much relieved as matters settled down again. Jane had clearly felt guilty at disturbing her parents and needed to be relieved of the burden of that guilt. It also seemed to make sense to the girls when their mother talked about the difference it made to the whole family now that she was out at work. In the parents' mind a crucial shift had occurred: the shift from trying to find someone to blame, to trying to understand. The bickering where each parent found fault with the other had yielded to a co-operative attempt to sort things out.

Dreams and nightmares

Who knows, Jane may have had problems going to sleep because she was afraid of bad dreams, especially while she felt she was upsetting the whole family. Bad dreams, sometimes very bad dreams, are common amongst four-year-olds. This is partly related to the way in which they hold on to a kind of belief in magic, which again relates to the way fact and fantasy are not fully differentiated in their minds. It is no accident that fairy tales are popular with small children. Many fairy tales are the very stuff of children's nightmares. In their nightmares or their bad dreams appear wicked versions of their parents; grown-ups who in another guise are big, helpful, protective figures are also seen as giants looming over their lives, twice as tall as they are. Mothers turn to wicked stepmothers or witches; baby brothers and sisters (real or imaginary) appear as horrible little gnomes or beastly animals.

It is not necessary for a child to have had exceptionally bad experiences for bad dreams to occur. At this age, as I have mentioned before, children are trying to sort out their feelings of love and hate, and they are subject to all kinds of rather primitive emotions. All children, for example, become very angry with their mothers from time to time – perhaps more angry at an unconscious level than they show in everyday life. Although Jane was being an awful nuisance, she was not obviously angry with her mother. It may well be that in her dreams her anger threatened to emerge, and a sort of hated version of her mother came into her dreams as a nasty witch.

Fears and fantasies

Closely linked with bad dreams are all sorts of imaginary fears (again, of course, a possible reason for Jane's not staying in bed – she may have been frightened when alone, even if she couldn't put her fear into words). Peter, whose washing-machine broke, was haunted by fears about the lavatory. He hated the noise it made when you pulled the chain. He had funny ideas about skeletons and goblins coming back up the pipe. Here we see the way in which four-year-olds still tend to invest their poohs and pees with magic significance. Instead of being able to think of them as just rubbish, they feel they have importance. Peter seemed to think that with his rubbish he also got rid of feelings and thoughts he didn't like – only they came back to haunt him!

The way in which stories or imaginings are not clearly differentiated from real life is shown when we see how a picture in a book can become so intensely frightening for a four-year-old. James's elder brother Dan had a book called *The Story of Beowulf* about the Viking hero who slays the monster Grendel. There was a horrid picture of Grendel, stalking over the mere with a cudgel in his hand, his mouth open to show yellow fangs. James was terrified by his picture but couldn't stop looking at it. No doubt it was in some way connected with his quite fierce feelings about his elder brother. The point here, though, is that James half expected Grendel to come to life, perhaps at night, and come to get him and eat him up. Nor did James fully believe that Grendel was only in a story and had never existed. To James the world of the imagination was as real at times as the world of everyday life. Of course, we have to remember that this is true of nice things as well as nasty ones, and that the four-year-old throws the light of the imagination over his good experiences which gives them a marvellous colour. James's experience of Christmas was as wonderful as his experience of Grendel was dreadful.

Behaviour problems – tantrums

What about four-year-olds on those occasions when they are really hard to manage? Perhaps the first thing to say is that a child in a tantrum is finding himself hard to manage. An explosion of rage can be an expression of despair. Indeed, we as adults on the receiving end often feel despairing too. A series of tantrums, like an outbreak of wetting or soiling in a child who may long have been toilet-trained, is a sign that the child's emotional system is somewhat overloaded. Feelings are bursting out of him or her; these feelings cannot be transformed into words and conveyed to others; they can only be expelled.

Here we touch again upon the importance of language. Certainly a child who is "all over the place", disobedient, and contrary probably doesn't know exactly what's the matter. But it is well worth while talking to him or her about it. Distress is being conveyed, but distress without increased understanding. The general rules for trying to locate and identify the source of the trouble still apply; by this I mean trying to take an overall look at the child's life and seeing what may be a source or sources of trouble and addressing that by thought, discussion and action.

Sometimes it is extremely useful to have another person to add a fresh point of view to a problem that may have got stuck. Somebody from outside may see things which people inside the difficulty just can't observe. Jonathan arrived with his mother at the doctor's surgery. His mother produced all sorts of worries and complaints about him; he wouldn't do what he was told, he messed things up, he wouldn't eat properly, he woke up in the night . . . and finally, he was afraid of balloons! "Afraid of *balloons*?" queried the doctor. Yes, Jonathan was. He was afraid of them in case they burst. He was also afraid of all unexpected loud noises; of cars back-firing, of Guy Fawkes day, of thunder claps, of doors which slammed in the wind, of bomb reports on the television, of things falling down – an absolute flurry of fears. The doctor felt nonplussed. Because she couldn't for the moment think what else to say, she said, "And how is your husband these days?" "Oh," said Jonathan's mother, "getting along, but it's taking such a time." The doctor saw that Jonathan had got very still and attentive. Could it be that he didn't really know his father was ill, that he had contracted a serious and unpleasant viral infection which left him unable to work for the time being, weak, apathetic and at home? "Jonathan must be worried about his father," said the doctor. She saw Jonathan's gaze swivel directly at her. To cut a long story short, it transpired that although everyone had taken it for granted that Jonathan understood about his father's illness, nobody had really explained it to him. He had been left with simmering worries. Actually, his mother had thought that he was both too young to notice and too young to worry. But he was worrying. He was deep down afraid that something ghastly, unexpected and frightening – a thunderclap – would happen. In ordinary language, which Jonathan might not have been able to formulate, he was afraid that his father would die. This tied up with his four-year-old rivalry with his father, and his four-year-old belief in magic. In a way, he wondered whether his wish to have Mum all to himself and to be quietly rid of Dad had worked! Dad seemed to be in a bad way. Was it his fault? What on earth had he done?

With the doctor's mild intervention, suggesting that Jonathan should be told his father was ill but was getting better, there was a lightening of Jonathan's spirits. We tend to think of depression as an adult emotion, but it can be felt at any age. The doctor asked Jonathan's mother to get her husband to come along for an extra check-up. She thought she might mention that Jonathan was worried, but in the event she didn't need to. The whole question seemed to be freed up. Jonathan's father spontaneously mentioned Jonathan's difficult behaviour and linked it to the fact that he hadn't been able to do what he would have liked with his son. Gradually the more exaggerated signs of Jonathan's anxiety died away and as his father recovered family life went on in an ordinary fashion. To an outsider the connection between Jonathan's behaviour and the family trouble had been obvious; to an insider without the intervention, not.

Eating difficulties

Eating difficulties are probably no more nor less prevalent at this age than at any other. As always, the child who refuses food or who is full of fads and fancies is a source of anxiety and irritation to those who care for him or her. Food is such a basic necessity that the threat of refusing it conjures up the ghosts of malnutrition and starvation. If you don't eat, you die: this idea rings in the backs of our minds even when we know that a child can last indefinitely on a fairly slender diet.

This book cannot hope to pinpoint why one particular child – perhaps yours – doesn't eat or doesn't eat well. It may sound repetitive, but yet again we have to look for what a sign of distress like going off your food really means. It is a sort of communication: the test of that is that it does communicate; it communicates anxiety, fear, anger, all those feelings which it evokes in mothers and fathers. In each individual case we must look for what's going wrong. An extreme case may help to show how this problem can contain a great deal in the way of meaning. A little girl from the Far East, an orphan, was brought to Italy and adopted by an Italian couple; they called her Livia. Livia developed severe eating difficulties while yet thriving in other ways and becoming attached to her new father and mother. Now you might say that of course she found food a problem; how entirely different the food of her new home must be from her old! A cultural problem, you could say.

However it was a cultural problem which went deep. Not only did the food seem to symbolise all that Livia found new, alarming and indigestible about the change in her life. She also showed by the violent way in which she sometimes

63

clamped her hand over her mouth or vomited back some food that she actually felt the food was terrifying and poisonous. At this time she was being a good, biddable little girl in other ways. Only as her confidence in her new family increased did she start to be more difficult and distressed. As she settled in, she was more able to dare to show more anger, antagonism and fear as well as more curiosity, liveliness and sparkle. When Livia got more in touch with the whole range of feelings that her adoption had aroused, and felt that her adoptive parents could tolerate her feelings without getting rid of her, her terror stopped being focussed on the food. She gradually began to eat in an ordinary way. Of course, it had been no good asking Livia why she couldn't eat. She simply didn't know. But food had turned bad on her; it had come to mean something dangerous instead of something necessary and delicious.

James, mentioned earlier, who had an elder brother Dan and who relied on being the charming baby until he was about four or five, had less severe eating problems, but more longstanding. James's problems were tied up with his partial refusal to grow up. He had been hard to wean; finding new foods he would accept was a trial from the very start. James hated lumps; he hated strong flavours; he didn't like things which were chewy or crisp or crunchy or tough. Basically, he liked cereal and pasta, mashed potatoes, yoghourt with perhaps a little chicken or a sausage. People told his worried mother that he looked fine. So he did. But she knew very well that something was a bit wrong. It was a relief to the whole family when James, tipped into the world of nursery and of school, eventually found the resources to make some essential steps in independence. Instead of charming the birds off the trees, he asserted himself, discovered different aspects of his own character and started to eat school dinners including the lumps.

Hyperactivity

Hyperactivity is a current term for restless, over-excited unhappy behaviour. A child may look lively, but it is a sort of false liveliness, an attempt to cheer up and infuse life into a difficult situation. Often it means that a child dare not keep still and think for fear of the thoughts which might arise. Of course, if your child has been diagnosed hyperactive you will have to listen carefully to medical opinion. But it is probably as well to keep looking for worries and emotional causes while at the same time following other lines of investigation. Children are often investigated for allergies and put on various diets if they are diagnosed hyperactive. Allergies are important and must be treated. But they can connect up with how a child feels, and the feelings need consideration too.

Masturbation and sexual play

Children often do masturbate. It frequently seems that they would like to lose themselves in sensation rather than follow their thoughts, and parents notice that masturbation increases under stress. Children tend to abandon it round about school age, and with a certain relief: it seems to produce as much tension as it resolves.

Sexual play falls into two rough categories: the more casual and the more driven. Children are, as we have already seen, curious about grown-ups, about how they differ from children, and about how babies are made. In their researches they may well look at each other's bottoms and try to see how they are made. Such investigation is usually a bit of a disappointment. You can see at a glance how a boy differs from a girl ("one plain, one fancy", said one child: "one sensible, one silly", said another rather sniffily). But the mystery of how babies are made remains. Indeed, creation always remains a sort of mystery and can never quite be fathomed. No matter how you poke about and look at another child's bottom, you will never find out as much about creativity as you will from thinking about symbolic forms of renewal like the seasons, or about stories and pictures.

The more relentless and driven forms of sexual play are more worrying. If a child at nursery is very determined to hang about at the toilets and look at everyone without pants on, or if he or she seems truly full of sexual information and preoccupations, it is time at least to query things. We have to remember that while the current anxiety about "child sexual abuse" concentrates on actual criminal acts, there are many lesser, non-criminal forms of over-stimulating children. Children who have not been protected from grown-ups' sexual activity, and who are stirred up and bewildered by having seen adult films or adult sexual behaviour, often enact this. They need to be noticed, because they need attention and possibly protection.

CHAPTER FIVE

MISFORTUNES

Telling the truth

What was touched on earlier about answering children's queries truthfully is very relevant when it comes to misfortunes in the family. Secrets are probably the most worrying things of all: our imaginations can provide worse things than most realities. If a child thinks that a matter is unspeakable or unthinkable, it can affect the whole way his or her mind works as he or she attempts to avoid talking about or even thinking about this hideous unnameable catastrophe.

Going to hospital; being ill

Parents often find that if a child is seriously ill – enough to warrant admission to hospital – there isn't much time to think about the best way to describe or explain what's happening. You have to do the best you can. This leaves children, and parents too, with a backlog of processing to perform. Children need to reflect on a difficult experience and to have a chance to digest it.

Even a minor hospital emergency can need a lot of thought. When Nicholas cut his lip he had to have stitches in it. His mother helped the nurses to hold him while the doctor sewed it up. Although it was an excellent thing for Nicholas to have his mother there, he somehow saw her, in his bewildered state, as helping the doctor to hurt him. It took a lot of going back over it in subsequent weeks before he began to come to terms with the concept that sometimes what is good for you has to hurt you, and the other concept that if you don't face this nasty thing now you may be sorry later. A stitched lip now is better than an ugly scar in years to come.

Sometimes hospital intervention, especially surgery, in infancy, leaves a legacy that wants investigating at a later stage. Gavin's parents noticed with discomfort that he was forever fiddling with his penis. Only when they went to discuss this with a child psychotherapist did they realise that his anxiety was the direct descendant of surgery he had had as a toddler. He needed to know all about his earlier operation and to think it over before his hitherto nameless anxiety was laid to rest.

Divorce

Divorce or separation between a child's parents has its own special difficulties when a child is only this age. Most children, it has to be said, are disturbed by the idea of parents separating: what they would like is the often impossible solution of the parents to stay together and get along beautifully. Because a four-year-old is naturally self-centred, and finds it hard to imagine that parents have a relationship independent of him or her, it's difficult to explain that mummy and daddy don't want to stay together although they are both still fond of him. But the attempt must be made to explain. Even if all one can do is to acknowledge that children can't always understand why grown-ups act as they do, it is essential to tackle the subject rather than to veil it in secrecy. At least the path will be clear for the child to see that a part of each parent loves him and in reasonable circumstances he can feel that they can co-operate in his best interests.

Where there are practical arrangements over such matters as access visits or shared care of a child, it is essential to be as clear as possible in explaining these: it is also much better if a regular pattern of visits or care can be established and kept to. While Vicky and Jake's father, who was separated from their mother, used to pop in when he felt like it, the children were kept in a constant state of miserable unease. They would far rather their parents had stayed together: or perhaps it is truer to say that they would have preferred it if there had been no need for the separation. With the natural egocentricity of small children, who think their parents revolve around *them*, both Vicky and Jake kept wondering what they had done to upset things. When their father re-appeared at odd times, it was as though things were back as they used to be before the break-up. Perhaps it wasn't true? Perhaps Mummy and Daddy were going to say that this rather horrible time was over? Perhaps Daddy would come home for good? Alas, there was no question of that: their parents had decided that the relationship had been a mistake, and their father was well on the way to finding a new partner. It was cruelly disappointing in some ways for Vicky and Jake to have to realise that the old days had gone for good.

However, it was better that they should mourn their old life and start a new one rather than that they should be in a state of bewilderment and dashed hopes. When a clear structure was worked out, a pattern of so many evenings and weekend days with Daddy, it helped Vicky and Jake to see that things were really different now. And of course it also reassured them: no matter how forlorn they felt over losing their parents' former relationship, they had a growingly solid feeling that they would lose neither parent altogether. They could start to trust the new way of life when it was regular and reliable. Also their parents, both in different ways, had realised that the children needed things to be explained and re-explained. All anxiety-provoking situations need this, as I shall say again further on. I am not talking about repeating things mechanically; I mean that when children are nervous, anxious, worried about what is happening they cannot take in explanations all at one go. Matters need approaching and re-approaching, thinking about more than once.

Death in the family

Not many four-year-olds are called upon to mourn the death of a parent or a sibling, but it does happen. More, perhaps, know the loss of a grandmother or grandfather, or of another significant person. In these sad circumstances it is not possible to get it right. We are all improvising and stumbling along. Most people nowadays realise that to fail to talk to children about a death in the family is to leave the child alone with his questions and grief at a time when he, like anyone else, needs company. However, it is easy enough to say this and harder to do it when the adults themselves are burdened with grief. Children may be ignored at a time of family mourning. In the case of one terrible car accident, where a child was killed and the mother badly injured, it was some time before anyone realised that the unhurt girls, who had been taken in by neighbours, had never been told that their little sister was dead. This was after her funeral, to which they had not been taken. They were perhaps too young for that, but at five and four they were certainly well able to comprehend much of what was going on. They were becoming scared and withdrawn. Reality, though dreadful, was in a sense preferable to their imaginings. They had needed to get started on the slow and painful process of grasping the fact that their sister would never return – a fact that children of this age find it especially hard to assimilate. Their imagination, the power of their fantasies, are so strong that time and again their wishes over-ride reality and we see them cling to the belief that a dreadful event hasn't happened, that a dead person is still alive.

In our earnest desire to help children with grief by talking about the dead person, we must be sensitive; to go to the extreme of forcing the topic on unwilling ears is no help. Waiting for the moment, being receptive to the child's overtures are probably the best approaches once the main task of tackling the sad question and explaining it is over.

Indeed, with any sort of misfortune, this is a safe general policy. Whether the unhappy event has been an accident, an operation, a bereavement, a divorce or any other family disaster, it is best to take the discussion of it at the child's pace. There needs to be some process of facing up to what has happened, some occasion where it is explained that Granny has died, that Daddy is ill, or whatever may be the central event. Then, after that, we have to be alert for times when the child would like to talk about it again. We need to watch for signs of disturbance – bedwetting, bad dreams, bad behaviour – and think to ourselves that these are probably related to the insecurity following something which has shaken the child's trust in his or her parents' power to protect. Perhaps, if it can be done delicately, it may be a good idea to see these disturbances as signals to talk a little more about the sad event. Or we may simply need to take the opportunity given by a quiet and intimate moment to return to the question. Getting over something like this takes a long time for a four-year-old just as it does for older people. You hear people say, "Oh, they forget so quickly", but common experience tells us this is not really true. Before children can lay aside a painful experience and get on with their lives there has to be this process of assimilation.

Parents' problems

Nobody really needs me to tell them that parents' own problems rub off on their children. I have already mentioned briefly that children need what protection we can afford them from the undiluted force of adult conflict and emotion. Even when we do our best, when children do not witness too much that is disturbing, they still are sensitive to their parents' state of mind. This is because a small child needs to be in intimate mental contact with his caregivers. We saw earlier how anxious Jonathan became about his father's illness, and the same factors operate when a parent is not ill but in distress. Oliver was taken to see a child psychotherapist because his mother said he had suddenly become unwilling to leave her, disliking the nursery he formerly enjoyed, insisting on being in her bed every night, rebelling against being left with a well-liked baby-sitter. As the mother was encouraged to describe their life together, it became clear that for her the idea that four-and-a-half-year-old Oliver would go to school in the Autumn was most upsetting. It signalled a separation between them, and a growing-up for Oliver. This in turn brought back some unresolved unhappy questions about loss in Oliver's mother. She was divorced and had clung to Oliver, shielding herself from mourning the failure of her marriage. It was plain that Oliver was a worried little boy, but also that he was concerned for his mother. It was arranged that Oliver's mother should have some meetings with the worker on her own to think about her own problems; it was impossible to tell at the time whether Oliver was disturbed or just naturally anxious. It proved eventually that when his mother's disturbance died down, Oliver was free to enjoy nursery, sleep in his own bed and to look forward to school.

CHAPTER SIX

LOOKING AHEAD

The next step for a child in Britain is the dramatic and important one of going to school. Some schools have nursery classes; some infants' schools take children at four-and-a-half. So one way and another school is in the minds of British four-year-olds. But whether it is called "real" school or something else in different countries, the kind of provision made for children of this age always caters for the particular pre-occupations of the age-group. Whatever stage a child has formally reached in the society in which he or she lives, as the fifth year passes and the child says good-bye to being four, new developments gleam in the distance.

Around five and six gradual changes will come over our four-year-old. The child who faced inward, towards the family, who converted all groups into family-type groups with the children relating to adults first and to children second, is growing into the child who faces outwards and who will distance himself or herself a little from the earliest passionate family involvements with mother or father. Something is fading as five years old comes up. It will not be seen again until puberty and adolescence. Some degree of intensity cools a little and we can see the school child emerging.

At the end of the Winnie-the-Pooh stories all the animals (who are sort of toys come to life) get the feeling that Christopher Robin is going away. They go to see him and "they all said 'Hallo', and felt awkward and unhappy suddenly, because it was a sort of good-bye they were saying, and they didn't want to think about it". And then Christopher Robin and Pooh go off together into the forest, and Christopher Robin says how what he likes doing best is Nothing . . . and then "suddenly" Christopher Robin changes gear and starts to talk about "people called Kings and Queens and something called Factors, and a place called Europe, and an island in the middle of the sea where no ships came to, and how you make a Suction Pump (if you want to) and when Knights were Knighted, and what comes from Brazil". Now this jumble of school-like stuff is rather old-fashioned and not what children learn about now; but there is a truth here. From the "doing Nothing", a time stretching back into infancy where time and place didn't mean very much, where people and feelings mattered most, children move with Christopher Robin to an interest in objective things, in a slightly different kind of learning, in society at large. Of course, we give our children a bit of a push. Christopher Robin says to Pooh, "I'm not going to do Nothing any more." "Never again?" asks Pooh. "Well, not so much. They don't let you."

Interest is going to shift just a little from the inner world to the outer. Both worlds will always co-exist and relate to each other in a vital way. But by the end of the time a child is four he or she has achieved a clearer and more reliable idea of what reality is: whether it is the inner reality of the imagination or the outer reality of the external world, he and she knows which it is and can differentiate between them.

FURTHER READING

Making and Breaking of Affectional Bonds, John Bowlby, Tavistock Publications, London, 1979

Playing and Reality, D. W. Winnicott, Tavistock Publications, London, 1971

Child's Talk, J. S. Bruner, Norton, 1983

Through the Night, Dilys Daws, London Free Association Books, 1989

Thinking About Parents and Young Children, Martha Harris, Clunie Press, 1975

Our Adult World and Its Roots in Infancy, Melanie Klein Collected Works. Penguin, 1991

HELPFUL ORGANISATIONS

Young Minds/The National Association for Child and Family Mental Health, 22A Boston Place, London, NW1 6ER (Tel. 071 724 7262)

In conjunction with the Child Psychotherapy Trust:

Exploring Parenthood, Latimer Education Centre, 194 Freston Road, London, W10 6TT. Parents Advice Line: 081 960 1678 (from 10 a.m. to 4 p.m.)

Gingerbread Association for One Parent Familes, 35 Wellington Street, London WC2 (Tel. 071 240 0953)

The Pre-School Playgroups Association, 61–63 King's Cross Road, London, WC1X 9LL (Tel. 071 833 0991)

Nursery and Pre-School Information Line, PO Box RB, London W1A 4RB (Tel. 0874 638007)

Play Matters/National Toy Libraries Association, 68 Churchway, London, NW1 1LT (Tel. 071 387 9592). Information available about loans of expensive toys that the child will grow out of and for advice about toys as well as toys for children with special needs and multicultural toys

Action for the Sick Child, Argyle House, 29–31 Euston Road, London, NW1 2SD (Tel. 071 833 2041)

Under-Fives Counselling Service, Tavistock Clinic, 120 Belsize Lane, London, NW3 5BA (Tel. 071 435 7111)

UNDERSTANDING YOUR CHILD

ORDER FORM FOR TITLES IN THIS SERIES

Send to: Rosendale Press Ltd., Premier House
            10 Greycoat Place, London SW1P 1SB

Price per volume: £5.75 inc. post & packing

Understanding Your Baby by Lisa Miller	. . . . . copies
Understanding Your 1 Year Old by Deborah Steiner	. . . . . copies
Understanding Your 2 Year Old by Susan Reid	. . . . . copies
Understanding Your 3 Year Old by Judith Trowell	. . . . . copies
Understanding Your 4 Year Old by Lisa Miller	. . . . . copies
Understanding Your 5 Year Old by Lesley Holditch	. . . . . copies
Understanding Your 6 Year Old by Deborah Steiner	. . . . . copies
Understanding Your 7 Year Old by Elsie Osborne	. . . . . copies
Understanding Your 8 Year Old by Lisa Miller	. . . . . copies
Understanding Your 9 Year Old by Dora Lush	. . . . . copies
Understanding Your 10 Year Old by Jonathan Bradley	. . . . . copies
Understanding Your 11 Year Old by Eileen Orford	. . . . . copies
Understanding Your Handicapped Child by Valerie Sinason	. . . . . copies
Understanding 12–14 Year Olds by Margot Waddell	. . . . . copies
Understanding 15–17 Years Old by Hélène Dubinsky & Jonathan Bradley	. . . . . copies
Understanding 18–20 Year Olds by Gianna Williams & Beta Copley	. . . . . copies

Total amount enclosed: £. . . . .

Name . . . .

Address . . . .

. . . . Post code . . . .